The Post Office Murals Restored

Also by Robert B. Shaw

Comforting the Wilderness (Wesleyan, 1977)
The Wonder of Seeing Double (Massachusetts, 1988)

THE POST OFFICE MURALS RESTORED

Poems by

Robert B. Shaw

Copper Beech Press

Acknowledgment is made to the editors of the publications in which several of the poems in this book first appeared: *Chronicles* ("Home Repair," "Scene from Childhood," "Fanlight," "Serving the Purpose"), *Cream City Review* ("Parting Gift"), *Crosscurrents* ("Camera Obscura"), *First Things* ("Finding the Diary," "Wisteria"), *Kentucky Poetry Review* ("Wind at Night"), *The New Republic* ("An Aspen Grove"), *The New Yorker* ("Picturesque"), *Partisan Review* ("Advanced Research"), *Ploughshares* ("Degrees of Resolution"), *PN Review* ("Still Life: Eyeglasses on Night Table," "Waldeinsamkeit," "Selva Oscura"), *Poetry* ("Shut In," "To His Pulse," "The Bookmark," "Still Life: Belt on Bureau," "Last Days in Camden," "A Pair of Bookends," "Florilegium"), *Shenandoah* ("A Piece of Rope," "The Key," "At the Bait Store," "December Vespers"), *Southwest Review* ("The Pupil"), *Verse* ("The Leaning Tree"), and *Yale Review* ("The Post Office Murals Restored").

I wish to thank the National Endowment for the Arts for a fellowship that enabled me to begin this collection, and the Ingram Merrill Foundation for a grant that helped me to finish it.—R.B.S.

Cover: *The Pioneer*, by Winslow Homer (1836-1910). Copyright © 1985 by the Metropolitan Museum of Art. Amelia B. Lazarus Fund, 1910.

For information, please write the publisher:
    Copper Beech Press
    English Department
    Box 1852
    Brown University
    Providence, Rhode Island 02912

Library of Congress Cataloging-in-Publication Data
Shaw, Robert Burns, 1947-
    The post office murals restored : poems / by Robert B. Shaw.
      p. cm.
    ISBN 0-914278-63-0 (pbk. : alk. paper) : $11.00
    I. Title.
    PS3569.H3845P67 1994
    811'.54—dc20
                                             93-47142
                                               CIP

Set in Galliard by Louis Giardini
Manufactured in the United States of America
First Edition

for my mother and father

Contents

I

HOME REPAIR

Climbing up the rented extension ladder
on the way toward patching his own roof
he halted midway, taken a little dizzy,
holding tight a ridged aluminum rung
and steadying the shoulder bag of needments —
hammer, nails, a few split cedar shingles —
then went ahead, without a second stop
getting himself beyond his second story.
Although his cuff jerked back each time
he gripped another rung he never thought
of what was on the untanned underside
of his right wrist: modest, whitening scar
too well stitched to blaze much of a trail
back to last year's lapse of equilibrium.
Clean that rain-gutter next, he thought. Up top,
he leaned himself back on the low-pitched,
sun-warmed slope and looked around, no vertigo
to cope with, just a moment's sheer surprise
at seeing down below so many small things
docilely disposed, in such trim order:
lawn mowed, car washed and waxed, zinnias weeded.
He hadn't known that he had come so far.

SERVING THE PURPOSE

You know those shims you make by folding paper
over and over in a tightening square?
You jam one under a china cupboard's foot
to stop its rattling every time you pass.
It does the job, and you forget it's there.

But now, with the gigantic van
hugging the curb out front, premises
emptying systematically room by room,
standing in a corner out of the way
of burdened, grunting, shunting men you hired,
suddenly you see it, off duty and forlorn,
lying as if pasted to a floorboard.
To pick it up would just anticipate
the final sweep it waits for, harshly dinted
by its day in, day out stint of holding
steady the shelves of breakable, gilt-rimmed stuff
brought out only to gratify the in-laws.
Now with that load pampered into barrels
("Excelsior!" — the motto for all movers),
you peer along the bare floor and gauge the slant of it.
All those years the old beams went on settling.
And you, haven't you learned to settle for less?

SELVA OSCURA

Impossible to examine this blown-up
photograph of brain cells without nudging
one's own to scare up some comparisons:
first, we might think here is a line of glyphs,
scratched across a scroll with a reed pen
in emulation of the subtle tracks
on Nile mud of Ibis, the first scribe.
But how to read them? If we trace the hint
of the word *dendrite* back to its Greek root
we can proceed from there sans lexicon,
and know them for a close-ranked row of trees,
brooding in purple almost black along
a twilit ridge, long-rooted, stubby-limbed,
and winter-leafless: all the birds have flown.
The artfully stained slide and keen microscopy
that can show this much won't elucidate
seasonal stirrings that excite the sap
or the occasional lightnings that
flash havoc in the branches, leaving scars.
Landscape or language-scrap, we know the place,
the passage, though it still remains obscure.
For where but here could we have thought
to find ourselves? And how, if not in wandering
deeper and deeper into this dark wood,
lost and alone in the middle of our lives?

DEGREES OF RESOLUTION

Borrowing his grandfather's reading glass
the boy next door takes time to educate us,
summoning us for safety off the grass
to squat on concrete round his apparatus,

the tool aforesaid and a random sliver
of paper. Now he tilts the glass to catch
a single dart from summer's bursting quiver,
training it on his target as we watch

to see before too long a speck of tan
appear and widen, deepen, till a wisp
of flame in scrawls too speeded up to scan
wrinkles its victim to a blackened crisp.

An odd ambivalence lies in this lens,
conferring stature on the minuscule,
hot, throbbing lines that one old gentleman's
eyes aim to see as large and still and cool,

yet of this fiercer knack an equal master,
yanking a fiery stylus down to write
a message that can only spell disaster,
culling the darker potencies of light.

Disparate ways of demonstrating strength.
The boy babbles his lecture on the laws
of optics and combustion, till at length
we back away with mumbles of applause.

This young instructor could not yet suspect
how much our nodding at his Q. E. D.
masks an uneasy leaning to reflect
on two opposing modes of scrutiny:

one that enhances to its keenest power
the lambent fact's crimped mimicking of essence,
and one whose pyrotechnics may devour
the fragile platform of their incandescence.

Rival enlightenments beneath one roof —
has one flared up to see the other fade?
Ask the old man, whose uncorrected proof
sends him out now to claim his reading aid.

A PIECE OF ROPE

It was a bad place to be a boy scout.
Tract houses huddled low on concrete slabs,
razored lawns under the pelt of sprinklers
soaked to a spongy green all summer long.
There was no place for him to pitch a tent
or light a fire. His father was away
on another trip. His mother, by contrast,
didn't seem to want to go anywhere.
Nothing to do but earn more merit badges
by developing pre-industrial skills
as advocated by the *Boy Scout Handbook.*
He sat and fiddled with a length of clothesline.
For the next badge he had to learn to tie
eight knots, and all by feel. So, he could practice
either blindfold or in some pitchdark place.
Earlier he had tried his mother's closet.
The heat — it was July — and the packed fumes
of mothballs prickling out from garment bags
made him dizzy, and there was little room
for him on the floor hemmed in by all her shoes.
Lightheaded, lightstruck, looking for a spot
less airless (everywhere was pretty hot),
he stumbled to the patio and slumped down
on slates with ragged grass grown in between them.
(It was behind the house, not on exhibit.)

He laid the *Boy Scout Handbook* down beside him.
The cover illustration, though he'd looked
a thousand times at it, still caught his eye.
It showed a campfire in the woods at night,
with a troop elbow-crammed around it, listening
dutifully to the leader's woodlore, watching
smoke waver up, presumably not seeing
what someone with the book in hand could see:
the spectral figure of an Indian brave
hovering in a haze above their heads,
pale blue against the night sky's indigo,
part there and part not there, as if composed
at best of shifty things, like smoke and stories.
He guessed that this was meant to make him think
of the spirit of the wilderness or something.

He thumbed through pages to the knot diagram.
Overhand knots and square knots and half hitches
he could do, but what about the sheepshank,
bowline, or sheet bend? It would take some study.
After a few bouts with a kitchen towel
tied around his eyes he didn't bother,
but simply kept them shut. He knew his honor
was what he had at stake and, in this case,
honor was not too hard to satisfy.

And it was calming, hypnotizing, sitting
in his own private night with careful fingers
teaching the rope its tricks. He heard his mother
talking on the phone inside the way
she'd done ever since his father went away
on the latest trip. "No. How do I know
where he is this time or when he'll come home?
How do I know if he'll come home at all?
You know last time he said he almost didn't.
No, he doesn't call. That's different this time."
He was fumbling now; his touch was off.
He quit listening, clamping his eyes tighter.
Finally when his fingers found the loop
they needed, and he'd pulled his two ends snug,
he kept pulling, cinching the docile cord
brutally to itself. She had hung up now.

It was weeks after this that he woke up
wrenching loose from the last strands of a dream.
He was one of the scouts on the handbook cover,
but when he looked up, what he saw was no
heroic Native American but his father
leaning out of the blackness of the sky
like a new constellation, looking blue,
at once blurred and fluorescent, and unlikely
to wander down from up there any time soon.
His fingers were all twisted in the sheet
and he could hear his own voice in the dark
far away, saying over the names of knots:
throat seizing, timber hitch, lark's head, cat's-paw.
And all the rest, and none of them of much
use in the darkness he was camped in now.

WALDEINSAMKEIT

Stepping over a rusted
strand of wire topping
a half-dismantled stone fence,
I step from field to forest,

finding the shade at first a mere
sketchy crosshatching, more
felt on the skin as coolness
than seen as thickening shadow.

But soon by steady paces
it deepens into precincts
where the path is only lit
with molten pennies scattered

through the random, shifting
loopholes overhead,
a meager trail the sun leaves
as it goes down to darkness.

Going nowhere, meeting no one,
it is again the old new world
of Adam, uncompanioned
except for all the furred,

feelered and many-footed
pets he passed away his time
by giving proper names to.
Like him, they all pursued

strict vegetarian diets,
even — that was Eden — these
mosquitoes I'm now slapping.
This, and my own brash tread

are now the only noises —
the birds have stopped. I stop.
When I again start forward
a sudden thrashing rips

from a clump of brush beside me,
shocking as the heave
and slash of a machete.
I stop again, see nothing.

It must have been a squirrel
or chipmunk tired of sitting
rigid for so long, soundless,
racked by his nut-sized heart's

terrified red alert.
My own, big as my fist,
still races as the scurry fades
of panicked feet escaping,

leaving me here alone
and savoring the lesson,
something I should have known
and always keep relearning:

that they will never learn,
the small ones too quick to see,
not to be seized with fright
at the sound or scent of me.

DOUBLE FEATURES

(Philadelphia)

Those Fifties sci-fi / horror films we loved
to scare ourselves, each other, silly with —
they've ripened to a rich absurdity
that soars beyond the joyous trashiness
they started with, which even we could sense,
giggling, squirming, at climactic moments
showering our grandfather's knees with popcorn.
My brother always sat on his left side,
I on his right, so he could get a grip
on both of us if needed. Tense and tingling
even before the lights went down, we sat
on the edge of our seats, our sneakers glued
to the floor's residue of splattered Cokes,
bug-eyed, wild for sights to scare our pants off.

Not every sort of scare was satisfying.
Retreads of Dracula seemed a shade remote —
nineteenth-century, musty, with a cloak-
and-daggerish eroticism we
were still too young to be in tune with. But
out-and-out monsters were in full supply
to do the job, gore-hungry and impervious
to conventional weapons, as the hapless
gunnery experts always found. No mere
artillery assault could stop Godzilla's
warty-haunched, implacable parade
through downtown Tokyo, crumbling earthquake-proof
high-rises at every step while savoring
tram cars slung from his jaw like sausage links.

Such miscreants emerged from the earth's bowels
or the sea-deeps, their solitude or sleep
disturbed by submarines or atom-bomb tests,
and got their own and more back in disruption.
The Beast from 20,000 Fathoms capsized
liners and tankers with his tsunami wake;
Rodan, the giant pterodactyl, fanned
winds from his wings of supersonic speed

which had a way of knocking buildings flat.
(This was an especially cheap production;
we noticed for ourselves the cardboard sets,
canvas flapping from the air-demon's wing.)
In his less densely populated setting
The Creature from the Black Lagoon made fishbait
of the explorers who had dared profane
the slimed, malarial, Amazonian bayou
that he called home, and only faltered when
he fell in love with the heroine, who screamed
and fainted at the least glimpse of his gills.
His downfall was a bit like Caliban's;
the starlet, though, who quailed and quivered in
his finny-fingered grip was no Miranda.
He was one of the few who wasn't bullet-proof,
but he was hard to aim at in the water.

There were another lot, of course, who weren't
stumbled upon but shambled in themselves
on forays from the hostile outer dark,
such as The Thing, whose fairly human form
disguised the fact that he was chemically
a vegetable — which wouldn't have been bad
had he not had a thirst for human blood.
Identical in diet but more awful
because weirdly amorphous, was The Blob,
an ectoplasmic clot of ooze that grew
and gained a deepening tinge of red as it
agglomerated people and their pets,
beginning grapefruit-sized but at the end
bloated enough with carnage to engulf
a roadside diner. At this desperate juncture
it was found to be sensitive to cold.
So they quick-froze it, hoisted it and dumped it
into the Arctic Ocean: that was that.
The scientists who spent most of these films
scratching their heads and asking for more data
in the end had no choice but to fall back
on boy scout ingenuity, luring the foe
to bite high tension wires, or trip and fall

into some convenient volcano.
The message seemed to be: you didn't need
to know much, you just needed to think quickly.

My grandfather was useful: we could grab
his sleeve when 3-D fangs lunged from the screen,
and since he was a minister he glossed
portentous Bible references, titles like
The Giant Behemoth ("It's in the Book of Job.
But there it's a hippo, not a dinosaur").
He also told us where the robot twins
Gog and Magog got their names. To sit
uncomplaining through those witless, lurid
matinees when he didn't even care
for popcorn was, I now think, something near
to sanctity. And what comes back to me
more keenly than the rollercoaster peaks
and dips of fright and boredom on the screen
is how entirely safe we felt with him,
coming out on the chewing-gum-stuck sidewalk
after the double feature, stretching, blinking
like a pair of touseled owls awaking.

He gave us each a hand and trooped us off
to find a street car. Once we must have dawdled
and had to run, clattering up the steps
of the rickety elevated station
to catch the northbound car. He gasped and sat
himself down heavily and handed me
the newspaper to hold. His face was flushed,
and though the car was rattling on again
it seemed to me that I could hear his breathing.
He took from his suit pocket a pill bottle
I'd never seen, uncapped it, took a tablet.
I was scared now, in a new way, but why?
Slowly his color paled to normal while
I looked around for other things to look at —
out the window a huge billow of smoke,
a fire burning somewhere in the slums,
or across from us an unshaved man

with unlaced shoes who kept on drinking something
masked by a paper bag. I tried to make
a tune up from our clacking down the track,
but all that I could think of was a clock
stupidly wound too tight, ticking too fast.
Soon we were on a downgrade, then inside
a stretch of tunnel, deepening our noise,
sleeving us in strange light. In a matter
of minutes we were up and out again,
and somehow, though just minutes had gone by,
it was all right. Himself again, Grandfather
was asking what our next week's movie would be.
My brother read the sports, I read the funnies;
Grandfather laid the news across his lap
and didn't look at it. It was near dark
when we got to our stop out in the suburbs.
No tentacles had seized us in the tunnel,
no claw had reached from heaven to derail us,
and we were ready and willing to be scared
next Saturday. We hadn't seen anything yet.

THE PUPIL

"darkness visible"

Dead center of
an archer's target,

black spot, a pirate's
presage of doom,

entrance agape
to a mountain tunnel —

what is it waits
on the other side?

Autodidact
of light's devices,

are you taken in, ever,
by what you take in?

You say you see,
but I see through you.

Floodlit, asquint,
diminished by day

you bide your time
till twilight offers

ampler scope
for dilated craving.

Avid aperture!
Gulper of shadows,

a wink of the sun
can only open

wider your goldfish-
mouth-like O,

as though you might
engorge all darkness,

compound, resolve it
to inner night,

make what you see
your property

(the world denuded
of color's pomps,

hardly worth having,
but never mind).

Sunset; see,
in the narrowing field

obscure forms, tranced
hypnosis victims,

troop to your yawning
hatch to be processed.

Plunge them deep
in your ritual bath

of brine; behold
their glints of struggle

as down they sink.
Ripples, dissolvings;

they leave your surface
limpid and staring,

dazzled with so much
savagely hid,

so much still moving.
Lower the lid.

AT THE BAIT STORE

Compact, uncomplicated, this is how I wish
the world could be. The only store in town,
it stocks whatever anyone would need
to stay alive, and then some — and displays it
all in one wide, dim, wooden-shelf-lined room.
Stepping past kids chugging Cokes on the porch
I jangle the strap of sleighbells nailed to the door
and find myself beguiled by — not abundance,
but something one might call sufficiency.
Groceries, of course, but also seeds
in case you'd rather try to grow your own,
useful spools of twine, a lot of different
sizes of screws and bolts and other hardware,
plastic kites and raincapes, sunhats, snowshoes,
brooms, bandaids, ballpoint pens and glue.
Not to mention all that angling gear
that keeps the summer people popping in,
bobbers and sinkers, line, and loads of hooks.
It's all a little cluttered, but just learn
the whereabouts of each one-shelf department
and you can feel the calm of categories
soothing the mind (almost as good as fishing).
Why couldn't we live here, not just spend a week?
Like the couple of indeterminate age
who own the place, both quiet, both beneath
the low-watt lights seeming a little dough-faced
as if they never had to go outside,
only upstairs (there is a second floor,
where they must — an odd phrase — live at night).
While he counts out change with a shy smile
I can imagine it: how, with the cardboard sign
flipped around from OPEN to CLOSED, he pads
down for a can of tomatoes she'll be cooking,
sidling past the cash register's silence
and past the cooler where in plastic cups
of peat moss the night crawlers hibernate,
barely twitching in plugs of humus, moist
coils kept for some fair morning's hook.

CAMERA OBSCURA

It was almost too hot to move that morning.
They made love anyway, the window shade
lifted a crack to let in what little air
was stirring, or say rather simmering.
Starred with sweat, they slid apart at last
and noticed something else had found a way
through the slim aperture: a perfect image
of the sunstruck other side of their street,
spread on the white wall opposite the window
in a thin, true-colored panorama which
(as if it wasn't already odd enough)
was upside down. Everything the window
customarily framed hung topsy-turvy:
liquor and grocery signs stood on their heads,
roof antennas dangled like bare coathangers,
and heavy drops that wept from air conditioners
rushed up instead of plummeting, like morning
dew racing to congregate in clouds.
(They couldn't see — it was out of the picture —
the sidewalk-ceiling those drops spattered on.)
This vision held for approximately ten minutes,
then faded out, leaving an ordinary,
featureless bar of white light on the wall.
They lay awhile wondering what the odds
would be of meeting such a sight again:
the angle of the sun, the set of the shade
would have to be precisely right, and they
themselves alert to serve as audience
for the unlikely, evanescent showing.
In the right place for once, at the right time!
How many happy accidents one summer morning
gathered and meshed on one hot city block
to make the humdrum world turn upside down?

FANLIGHT

A half-wheel glazed above the door:
six wooden spokes in shadow cast
increase their reach along the floor,
touching the hall's far end at last.

Deprived of full rotundity
and axle, too, on which to spin,
what else but solar energy
would fuel its daily journeys in?

Between these radiating lines
the pie-cut shapes of radiance fall.
Poured from the threshold, such designs
dazzle to shame the modest hall,

and set us squinting when our own
way in or out must cross their tracks.
Leaving the tiny torrid zone,
we feel its brand upon our backs.

You ask what all this adumbrates?
Some doors are slow to open wide.
Be hopeful; say "illuminates."
More of the same light waits outside.

LAST DAYS IN CAMDEN

I

Days of calm. An invalid's mild diversions.
The pony cart, his present from admirers,
has the lame oldster trotting gamely round
his down-at-the-heels neighborhood once more.
It puts high color back into his face.
Jaunts of a few blocks cheer him. Reins in hand,
he tastes the freedom of a few years back,
when he could ramble far out of town, and did:
say, down the coast on a sunny winter's day
to limp sturdily up and down the beach,
tolerably like the ones he wandered
mile on mile in his Paumanok boyhood
(or like one that slips into his dreams
night after night, its flat, deserted stretch
passive under the crash and yank of combers).

Summers were better still. Hospitable waters
beckoned him convalescent to the woods
back of the Staffords' farm on Timber Creek.
There he would cast his clothes aside and wrestle
with a young sapling, leaning his whole weight
against its springy stem, trying to feel
a green suppleness stealing by mere contact
into his dragging limbs.
                              He squelched in ooze
of his favorite rivulet, rinsed his mud bath off
in a clear spring, then sprawled in a camp chair
to take the sun, bucknaked but for a wide-brimmed
straw hat. Slate-colored dragonflies in pairs
hovered close to his nose, inspecting him.
Sometimes he broke the silence of the woods
by singing songs he'd picked up from the army,
or from the just-freed slaves. He made
the cedars ring, an American Silenus
loafing at ease in his triumphant, improvised
western New Jersey spa. Edenic hours
pencilled just as limpidly as they passed.
Casual daybook entries burgeoning into

Specimen Days. . . .

Taking a corner now
at a terrific clip, he lurches, chuckles,
chokes up on the reins. His friends wonder:
had he ever driven before? A graybeard child,
thrilling to a new toy . . .

Then later strokes
cut back his territory. His rig idles.
The little horse, with no way to earn his oats,
is sold at last. His outings, much less frequent,
now have to be less heady. Warren, the wiry,
mustached, cardiganed, indispensable nurse,
bumps him down to the docks in a rickety
rattan wheelchair. There he watches coal boats
smudging by, and the everladen ferry
he once rode back and forth on half the night
just to look up at stars. Tug boats mewl,
cargoes jostle on and off of barges.
All rivers are one river. Now he looks
blinking across the brown wash of the Delaware,
inhales, resigned, the air he calls "malarial."
Time to go back. His wheels jounce on pier planks.

II

His cramped house sits on Mickle Street, an area
destitute of charm and, frankly, destitute.
An upstairs front room, homely with iron stove
and sprigged wallpaper, serves as bedroom, study,
and a salon to bands of devotees
come to receive the latest oracle.
Brash young men, the anti-Victorian vanguard,
herald his birthdays with fanatic zeal,
cosseting him with oysters and champagne.
He indulges them. He indulges himself,
as far as strength permits. Idolatry
carries vexations, though. He sags a bit
under the growing burden of their hopes
for the wonderful, unbuttoned twentieth century

that he won't live to see: a world redeemed
from priestcraft and hypocrisy, made happy
by universal suffrage and free love.
Mail will go faster (just the other day
someone sent him a little pasteboard box full
of orange buds, still fresh, from Florida).
Human relations will be governed by
the gospel of his verse and no doubt also
the wisdom of phrenology. He muses,
feeling his bumps with gentle, probing fingers.
Just as he was told: "Adhesiveness,
Amativeness, Self-Esteem, Sublimity"
all bulk large beneath his grizzled mane.

In between delphic interviews he dozes
in his big chair by the window, writes
snatches of verse, little squibs for the papers,
almost managing to ignore the reek
of the fertilizer plant across the river,
the chuff and rattle of the trains that pass
a hundred yards away and, when they don't,
on Sundays, sour Methodist steeple bells,
crass opponents of everybody's peace.
Papers and books heap round him on the floor.
He stirs them with his cane, or reaches down
now and again to riffle through the mess.
By a slow, unpremeditated system
of crossfiling, items migrate to the top.
Accolades from Swinburne, from Rossetti,
pleasant regards from Tennyson, fervent
declarations of love from female votaries
offering to conceive his child on some
fortunate mountaintop and save mankind.
Emerson's letter, lost for years, crops up,
tendering in its prim, Spencerian hand
thanks for the astonishing gift of *Leaves*:
"I greet you at the beginning of a great career."

III

Photograph after photograph, his countenance
gives nothing away. He knows and says it:
"There is something in my nature *furtive*
like an old hen!" How many prize eggs lie
clandestine in the hedgerows of the past?
His hooded, sunken eyes at last look back
and cannot see through his own snarled webs
to find those clutches lovingly concealed.
Nor can his biographers do better:
searches for the six illegitimate children
scattered supposedly through the south yield nothing.
A mystery unto himself and others,
he lets the camera catch him if it can.

Less than a year before his death he sits
a last time for his good friend Mr. Eakins.
Paints laid aside, the savage Philadelphian
stoops under his black hood, tweaks the bulb,
and frames Walt by the window in May sunlight.
A long exposure. But the subject is
accustomed to the discipline of sitting.
Here he is Prospero with his spells disowned,
or a Hasidic sage in contemplation,
or a retired Santa Claus who seems
half-transfigured in the window-light
which sets each wispy filament of blanched
prophetic beard to glowing. He leans back
against the darker, draping shagginess
of a wolfskin, wild mate to his repose.
Spring no longer lends heat to his flesh.
He waits here, well wrapped up, for what will come.

Waits with an old lover's tingling patience.
Whatever "furtive" (his word) human fumblings
he may have hid from others, from himself,
his true secret was something else, and hidden
like Poe's purloined letter, in plain sight.
Forget the baffled courtships of young laborers,

shy gifts of rings, and letters of endearment
tapering off as one by one the protégés
grew up, branched out, got married. This was not
what brought a skip and quickening to his pulse.
It was not sex but "heavenly death" which drew
his fascinated ardor all his life.
Faceless itself, reflecting all men's faces,
it held him, murmurous, many-lipped, enticing,
androgynous, a depth waiting unsounded,
into which one could slip without a ripple.
It overtook his soul in childhood,
saying its name to him on the night beach,
calling out in the tumbling of the waves.
Later it came back like a tide to steep
the rough-hewn hospitals of the Secession War.
Washed in the blood and tears of his new calling,
he sat by day and night beside the beds
of shattered soldiers, sponging at their brows,
writing their last words down in letters home.
Sometimes he helped to fold their finished hands
and walked behind the stretchers borne foot forward,
the cots already stripped for the new wounded.
Watchful, he marked the end as calm, maternal,
infinite in its welcome to desire.
This was the vision kept as counterweight
to every other force which stirred this kosmos.
So he declared his interest more than once.
Wildly out of context, for example,
in a prose dithyramb to democracy:
"In the future of these States must arise poets
immenser far, and make great poems of death."
Or is it out of context after all?
It may be just that longing for surcease,
a huge oblivion in or over nature,
which makes his writings most American.

IV

The deathbed scene, so cherished by an earlier
century when the practice was to ebb
and cozily expire at length, at home,
played itself out on Mickle Street with some
distinctive variations. Standing in
for the extended, hand-wringing family were
disciples trading off day and night shifts,
crank journalists, male nurses, amanuenses
jotting his few words down when he could not
manage his colored pencils any more.
Appetite failed in him. The last three days
he took nothing but small sips of milk punch.

After they moved him to "a water-bed"
(startling to learn they had a thing like that
in 1892) his ragged breathing
softened, and seemed to give him much less pain.
He heard the sound of water under him
swelling and lapsing, cradling his weight,
and gave himself up to it with a smile.
It was in keeping — wasn't it? — with his style:
ample, undulant, massing and lulling back,
penned simulacrum of the sea that shaped it. . . .
When he stopped breathing suddenly, his heart
("a very strong organ with him") continued
to beat ten minutes more. The camerados
watched him on his way to fathoming this:
"different from what any one supposed, and luckier."

II

SHUT IN

Like many of us, born too late,
(like all of us, fenced in by fate),
    the late October fly
    will fondly live and die

insensible of the allure
of carrion or cow manure.
    Withindoors day and night,
    propelled by appetite,

he circles with approving hums
a morning's manna-fall of crumbs
    hoping to find a smear
    of jelly somewhere near.

In such an easeful habitat
while autumn wanes he waxes fat
    and languorous, but not
    enough to let the swat

of hasty, rolled-up magazine
eliminate him from the scene.
    Outside, the air is chill.
    Inside, he's hard to kill.

Patrolling with adhesive feet
the ceiling under which we eat,
    he captures at a glance
    the slightest threat or chance,

and flaunts the facets of his eyes
that make him prince of household spies.
    And as he watches, we,
    if we look up, will see

a life of limits, like our own,
enclosed within a temperate zone,
    not harsh, not insecure,
    no challenge to endure,

but yet, with every buzz of need,
by trifles running out of speed.
>   One day he will be gone.
>   Then the real cold comes on.

PICTURESQUE

That farm just north of town
does little but subsist.
Tumbledown sheds, machines
peppered with rust: it means
another struggle to exist
is tiredly winding down.

After their stand of corn
is picked to the last ear,
they let the cornstalks stay
to bleach as pale as hay.
Signalling winter near,
beggared and blond, forlorn,

these come into their own
beneath a birdless sky,
and give the meager field
for once a second yield —
ingathered when the eye
sees beauty in the bone.

Opportunistic eye.
Eye of the passer-by.

THE BOOKMARK

Tending to lose your place?
At your age you may find
a sentence (like a name, a date, a face)
escapes the ranging mind.

Stray points can be retrieved,
to which end I'm engaged
to lie at length among them, interleaved,
until you'd have them paged.

I serve as well for that
as memory serves the young.
It's no great pain to tell you where it's at
by sticking out my tongue.

A PAIR OF BOOKENDS

Two little owls, twins down to a feather,
put in hours upholding Western Civ.
Curiously, what brought them first together
holds them apart — those words by which we live.

Centered on a black marble pedestal
each of them roosts upon his open book.
Never a hoot escapes their vesperal
calm as they brood, easy to overlook,

in a dull sheen of bronze and verdigris
guarding the upright, sober, classic row.
However distantly derived from trees,
such gathered leaves are all the leaves they know,

and would know better were they to explore
the sum of them, and not alone the ones
pinned open by their claws the while they pore.
Those folios they scan are blank and bronze,

empty reflections of their staring eyes.
I'd say they earn their space by weight and age
rather than endless hankering to be wise.
Wisdom is knowing when to turn the page.

AN ASPEN GROVE

All agitation, flinches, quiverings —
life is unrest among these skittish things.

Something gave them a scare once. In a flock
they scurried up this hillside nubbed with rock

until they reached this ridge, a firm redoubt.
Here they could take a stand, and face about,

catching their breath, still trembling. Where's their pride?
Glimpses of lily-livered underside

flitter for all to see; the merest breeze
triggers the timorous spirit of such trees

to make each leaf a manifest of fright.
Are they assailed with terror of the height

they cluster in? Or, still, of what below
routed them up the slope so long ago?

That river down there wriggles like a snake . . .
Why are we tempted, even now, to make

a link to legend? Manning their lookout, we're
tapping the veins of some far older fear

than any that would set us now astir.
And no, we're not afraid now. But we were.

AGAIN, CICADAS

Where were we when we heard that sound before?
Seventeen years ago these fervent minstrels,
newborn nymphs, slipped shyly underground,
while their progenitors, equally fervent,
filled summer with their bickering castanets,
clicked at a rate that rivaled the tense whine,
say, of a surgical saw cutting through bone.
Silent throughout their long novitiate
the young fattened on tree roots, served their term
as flunkies of Persephone's bedchamber.
Theirs is the longest life span of all insects,
if you can call this twilit mustering life.
But now, more than a decade and a half
outworn, they come to light, shinny up trunks,
shrug off their ragged dustcoats and flaunt wings;
all this accompanied by the ancestral music
years of muteness hone to so wicked an edge.
Noon is pressing down its stifling dome.
We cannot for the life of us remember
where, if we were together, we were sitting,
what we were thinking, feeling, or not feeling
when we were last regaled by the heady percussionists.
Isn't that all for the best? Oblivion
edits the past with a tact we've come to admire.
But periodicity still carries its pang
in pointing forward: when the next performance
batters the hot air certain trees will have gone
up in smoke, oh, ages ago, and some
who, as Thoreau said, warmed themselves twice,
first heaving the ax and finally poking
radiant ash in a blackening grate, will be
well beyond reach of that or of any heat.

MONARCHS

Enthroned on royal blue
Veronica, these two
itinerant potentates
survey their lush estates.
Day sinks to a drowse
as daintily they browse;
within their orb of flowers
the minutes might be hours,
an hour idling by
could rival all July
for slowness, stillness, heat.
The world is at their feet.

This settled state of things
is wishful thinking. Wings
that wave but to display
their poise in holding sway
will soon discover speed,
routed by pouncing need.
Rebellion in the North
will storm to sweep them forth
by ways they only know,
mourning, to Mexico,
finding a last resort
there for their exiled court.

But now they rule, at rest,
their jet and saffron crest
emblazoned on those vans
that each serenely fans.
Weed-pullers on their knees
pay tribute to their ease,
sensing the day is near
when they will not be here,
their sublime dynasty
a fluttering memory.
If memory holds worth
still on the hurtling earth
when the sedate regime
has fled and left supreme

hegemonies of ice,
let commoners think twice —
give the requisite nod
to the time's iron rod
but save their loyalty
for banished royalty.
When the war lords are slain
they will return to reign.

LUNAR ECLIPSE

She shows her brightest face
climbing the sky tonight,
then notices us edging out of place
and pilfering her light.

At first it turns her red
to find us ambling near:
could it be bashfulness or anger, spread
into her virgin sphere?

But soon her color's faded
into a paler bisque;
and now her crystal rim gives way, invaded
by our penumbral disc.

It glides aloft, occluding
all we can see of her.
So, yet again, a genius for intruding
defines our character,

and she, for once unable
to hold herself aloof
as famously had been her wont in fable,
looks down on no one's roof.

This cold, obscure conjunction,
performed, is quickly past.
We spin away, too dazed to feel compunction
at having thus trespassed,

but dragging shadow tracks
behind us like bad dreams.
Somewhere, through all of this, behind our backs,
the sun looks on and beams,

spotlighting her, still paler,
but firm in her fixed arc.
Whatever momentary shades assail her,
she dominates the dark,

and leaves us none the better
for this unlikely tryst.
Closing our eyes, we labor to forget her:
that cratered cheek we kissed,

feeling its ancient flaws
with apprehensions fed
by that bland, ascendant look which draws
the ocean from its bed.

THE LEANING TREE

Craning above the shallows of the lake
a birch tree tilts at forty-five degrees —
aberrant, ostracized by other trees
uprightly disengaged from this mistake.

Angling like a flag- or fishing-pole
but luring neither nibbles nor salutes,
this livid shaft, leaf-proud, disclaiming roots,
leans gamely after some far ebbing goal.

Mind sputters into motion, milling various
edgy expressions — "on the verge! — the brink!" —
captions imposed by one too prone to link
trumpery strands of ever more precarious

ponderings on these boughs. Their semaphore,
breezily minimal, only mimes the utter
singleness of their bent, a verdant flutter
finding no answer on the facing shore.

Can it be gesture, canted taut in search,
an attitude of beckoning or yearning?
Yield to that slant on things, and all discerning
hovers midway like this wrongheaded birch,

neither quite dancing loose the drag of fact
nor tethered snug in tangibilities.
Let figures bid for pathos as they please.
See how the tree abides their sleights intact:

anchored in earth the ripples keep eroding,
the roots have not yet floated from their grip
and license trunk to jut and leaves to dip,
leaving to us the words of loss and boding.

A RECORD PRICE

*(Adoration of the Magi, by Andrea Mantegna. Sold
to the Getty Museum for $10.4 million in 1985.)*

Going, going, gone . . . to Malibu.
The Infant's fingers couldn't span to hold
the heavy treasures which the turbaned crew
are wishing on him, weights of spice and gold,

yet as his Mother lifts him, up he lifts
a tiny hand, accepting all he sees,
flutters a blessing on the burnished gifts
and brings the star-struck Wizards to their knees.

Such modest, mighty gestures will command
the notice of the spieling auctioneer
and bring his gavel down. Whence understand
at what a price our peace was purchased here:

Seeking his own true image, this young Lord
discerned our likeness to him, all but lost;
and knowing too how it might be restored,
he made his bid, and never grudged the cost.

DECEMBER VESPERS

Evening is early, supper too.
Moving about and stacking plates,
we notice what the windows do
when outer darkness congregates:

which is, to make a wider show
of what we've had for company —
two candles, half-consumed. They glow
in not-so-dim facsimile

on black, impassive panes. They seem
to hover in the boreal air
beyond the glass, their pointed gleam
unbent by any winds out there.

Hung in a garden felled by frost,
what have they to illuminate?
Their aim and nature must be glossed;
so, of a mind to meditate,

we name them: lamps of a ruined shrine,
relighted after long disuse.
And while divided fires combine
to witness to this moment's truce

between the outdoors and the in,
we linger — less inclined to snuff
their votive lights than we had been.
Nights are already dark enough.

TO HIS PULSE

Taut, industrious little drum
tensed in the hollow of my wrist,
beating alert beneath my thumb,
nature ordains that you persist.

Even when sleep has swaddled half
the world and me with unconcern,
taps of your jungle telegraph
attend the planet's somber turn.

What's it about? The steady throb
of traffic through your narrow sluice,
a rich monotony your job
of marking time must reproduce.

On the canal around the clock
you signal with your brisk tattoo
the level reached within the lock,
drumming the vital cargo through.

That ebb and flow that you denote
returns in circles to its source;
and I, no rebel yet to rote,
am pleased to leave it to its course,

and pleased to make your paces mine,
once more to the pump and back.
Your sudden halt will be the sign
that I have left the beaten track.

III

THE KEY

Picking up one from the multitude ringing the maple,
I wonder why they call this thing a key:
with two stiff wings spread in a two-inch span,
green as a tree toad, it resembles more
a chloroformed, mounted specimen moth — or less
morbidly, I'd say, a model glider
(or fancifully, a Japanese parrot kite).
Aerial craft of whatever kind, it's fallen
victim decisively to gravity.
I let it drop. It lunges fatally down.
Ants on forays to the disaster site
in due time will convoy scraps of wing
off to their salvage depot for recycling,
but not before the cockpit at the center
blotches brown and rends itself to spill
out of its breached care the stunned bush pilot
who at first will skulk in the tall grass,
trying to get his bearings, dazed survivor
of still another unobserved crash landing.
Now how to get back up again? It hinges
on going underground, and finding there
hiding inside him what I see I've been
rummaging for myself, the elusive key
offering entry to the sun-crossed air
as it unlocks what aims within the seed
to make its long climb upward and be freed.

WISTERIA

Here it comes again,
after shamming dead all winter,
stretching, flexing, limbering, unleashing
hordes of feather-cut leaves that look
like dragon tongues, a silty river bronze,
before they flatten to assume
their summer-long, grass-emulating green.
Gone in a few days from dry
sticks and frizz to rampant, virid vine,
it fans out an advance guard
of tentacle-tendrils itching with intent
to get a purchase somewhere, anywhere,
by means of those unshowy but efficient
grappling hooks that stud
their wiry length like blunt, vestigial thorns.
It scrambles up and onward
always by spiralling round whatever
stands in its path — drainpipe, porch pillar, lawn chair —
but then, once anchored, corkscrews round
itself, amassing braided cables
of self-hugging self-satisfaction,
the conquering hero's doublejointed
pat on his own back, the unbridled
ego trip impelled by uppity sap
from deepset root to farthest outflung tip,
ecstatically, imperially
quivering toward its vegetal entelechy.
It's then I intervene, unshackle
the captive clothesline post, prune back
that onslaught to a standstill: several times
a summer hacking through the worst intrusions,
severity which seems but to encourage
further incursions.
                   Why not have an end,
enlist some two-handed engine to smite once
and smite no more? It must be that we need
each other, complementary claimjumpers
locked in contest through the drowsiest
spells of heat, continually rousing
each other to claw back ceded tracts

of still disputed territory.
                              And
it's worth it, too (I say, sweeping up heaps
of stemmy trash), to see how every May
before these rank, voracious leaves
abound, the blossoms burst from the bare wood
(prized by the Chinese for this, and prized by me),
fountaining down in beads of wistful blue
like droplets of spring's mild sky congealed.

FLORILEGIUM

A village crossroads; quaint, curb-hugging store.
Secondhand shelf of books: what have we here?
The Language of Flowers, by Mrs. L. Burke,
fetched down from its unobtrusive perch,
sits in the palm of a hand so delicately
you'd think it apt to flutter up and away
(if it could find a magic window open)
back to its heyday as a genteel maiden's
lexicon of the sweet codes of romance.

Look, the faded name of one who owned it
flaunts curlicues across the flyleaf: think
how eagerly she used this to construe
nosegays her young man sent her, blossom by blossom,
into the compliments he never quite
put into words as pretty as her thought
of what he thought of her. Of course he had
his own copy, an early gift from her.
Dutifully he consulted it, avoiding
Pink Larkspur ("Haughtiness") and Candytuft
("Indifference"), falling back on such safe bets
as Jonquils ("I desire a return of affection").
Or, as he grew in confidence, a cluster
of White Roses ("I am worthy of you").
If the bouquets became too large, she'd send
a handful of Scarlet Poppies ("Fantastic
extravagance") by way of mild reproof.

Courtship by flower telegram could take
quite a few growing seasons to be sure
that all that needed to be said was said.
To us it seems incredible, for nothing
dates faster than sentiment, except
perhaps iconoclasm. Could we salvage
any of these fair fancies for our use,
even as we forgo the parlor palms,
doilies, buttonhooks, gutta-percha collars
that furnished so unpassionately the lives
of those who spelled their yearnings out in petals?
Could we resume the perfumed ceremonies?

Small chance, seeing what makes the windowpanes
rattle just now — familiar, stuttering roar,
as teen bikers in denim gun it past,
boy/girl, boy/girl, rocketing off to pop tops
in the shade of the next cinderblock 7-Eleven.
Their dust-wake coats the facing cemetery's
plastic flowers with a brusque farewell.
Where are you when we need you, Mrs. L. Burke?
Hopeless, ever to dream that fast-lane crowd,
or even we, at our more measured pace,
would pause to crack the cipher of a tongue
dead as Etruscan. . . .

                                Ah, but turn the page.
Something unlooked for looks back shyly, pressed
midway through the book: a flower, in fact,
whose vital juices oozing out have left
a brownish silhouette, whose own slight form
is flatter now and drier than the leaves
it's hidden in so long. It's milky blue,
and, from its size and petals, began life as
a Violet. Which, the book says, bears the sense
of "Faithfulness." Somehow its mere survival
seems to endorse that meaning, not so different
from what those plastic blooms across the way
do their own best, in their own time, to say.

59

ADVANCED RESEARCH

A buzzer sounds. And now a voice, too bored
to reach for pleas or threats, broadcasts the same
old bulletin: the library will close
in fifteen minutes. I can hear a quickened
pummel of footsteps through the thin, rattling
ceiling, and I wonder what it is
holding me back from joining in that ratlike
scurry of desertion. Even more
pointedly, I wonder why I'm here.
This is a level of the stacks I've never
up to now been lost in — so far down
below ground it's in fact a sub-sub-basement.
Stingy luminosity meted out
by jittery ceiling tubes about to fail
helps even less than usual to scan
the titles mouldering on their metal shelves.

Really, it's like a mineshaft; I could use
one of those flashlight caps the miners wear,
I tell myself — when, sharply as a lightbulb
switching itself on, it comes to me:
the quest is at an end. Here in this section,
if I can only find it, is the book
I've been tracking for years, beginning seven flights up,
the book that waits to tell me everything
I'll ever need to know. It's worse than hopeless
without a call number; I'm about
to give it up when suddenly my eye
fixes on a particular cobwebbed spine.
Unbelievable luck — can it be trusted?
I pull it from its shadowed perch and turn
a flaking leather cover back, and find —
dust. The pages all have pulverized
like some poor pharaoh's mummy stripped
of grave-linen in a rough hunt for gems;
now at my feet a little heap of chaff
is all this long-sought volume has to show,
except for the one smaller leaf laid in
as afterthought, printed apparently
on paper more enduring: the errata,

noted without apologies as follows:

For "inessential parts" *read* "in essential parts."
For "god" *read* "goad."
For "construction" *read* "constriction."
For "near" *read* "fear."
For "father" *read* "farther."

Settling now for anything, I pocket it.
I have five minutes left to make the door.

PARTING GIFT

Last night when I walked our old friend out the door
the sky was glazed and patchy, like black ice,
and I could hear the late cars crackling past
over the crusty, packed and rutted snow.
She heard them too, and said, "Do you know what
you call that sound?" I wasn't thinking. "Crunching?"
"No! They *crepitate*. That's what my father
said when he heard the wagons in the winter
going down the pond road. He'd announce,
'They're crepitating.' Those were even colder
winters we had then, if you'll believe it."
I was happy to believe it, creaking
(crepitating!) down my none-too-well cleared path
to her immaculately cared-for car;
happy she didn't greatly need my elbow
(think of it: almost eighty and still driving),
happy above all to feel the air
tingle, the way it will, at the right word.

SCENE FROM CHILDHOOD

There was a farmer pushing a plow
over and over, around four walls.
Between each sight of him and the next
were tufts of flowers, a curious crop.
For the first seven years of her life
she found him working when she woke up.

He was in profile, hat pulled down,
face hardly showing, bent to his job.
His horse looked happier, stepping high
as if the field were no great chore.
His shirt was red, his pants were blue.
(The prancing horse and the flowers were too.)

When they ordered her up on hot afternoons
to (ugh) take a nap she would try to count
just how many times the man and his horse
were going over the same old ground.
She always fell asleep, of course,
before she got even halfway around.

They held to the same deliberate pace
except for once, when measles kept her
up in her bed, with her fever up,
and then the figures seemed to race;
not even the flowers stayed in place.
They fluttered and sighed in a parching wind.

When she got better the walls stood still.
It would have been when she was six or so.
They moved next year to another state,
leaving the farmer still in full stride,
horse high-stepping, flowers in bloom,
doing their best in an empty room.

For some new child moved in to stay
would all their labor exert such charm?
Would they go limp without her watching,
loaf in the shade and leave the farm ·
to weeds and weasels? She wondered, watching
farms whipping by on the white highway,

finding no answer for how many years
till now, when a harness jingle, a heavy
share ripping dirt have startled her ears.
Still in mid-furrow as she wakes up . . .
But nothing is there. Her walls are white.
They call it a day at the end of the night.

FINDING THE DIARY

Settling the estate, the lawyer said.
It seemed too grand a way of putting it —
bills to be paid, a bank account to close,
and finally her mother's house to sell
while her own, half-a-continent away,
sat waiting for her with its lights on timers
and neighbors dropping in to feed the fish.
Bare rooms show better, the agent said.
So she proceeded with the emptying out,
giving away most of her mother's things
to cousins for their already jammed parlors
and china cupboards, and arranged to have
one rug shipped that was too big for her car.
She even dusted, as she rarely did
at home, all the time hearing in her head
her mother's brusque, exasperated murmur
after the hired help was out the door:
"Nobody knows what clean is anymore."
Maybe, she thought, this last clean sweep would please her.
Working her way from room to thinning room,
sorting, discarding, labelling, she found
herself at last up in the attic broaching
some cartons not her mother's but her own,
packed away since she had gone to college
and her room had become the sewing room.
Sweaters gaudy with school insignia
and one, half-knitted, that she'd never finished
lay folded softly on some weightier things:
Bio and Chem notes, watercolor attempts,
the high school yearbook proving at a glance
that bliss lies in oblivion. Had she really
had names for all those eager faces inked
with urgings time had made inscrutable?
("Remember Halloween in junior year";
"Don't forget the fun we had in Art Club.")
She hurried past her own sweet, solemn picture,
then set the book aside to shuffle through
the last stack of papers when something smaller
slithered out of them in an even more
embarrassing bid for recognition. Had she

buried it there on purpose? Or just briskly
bundled it in with everything she wouldn't
want or miss when leaving home at last?
She could hardly believe that it had surfaced,
looking, unlike the rest of the sad items,
almost new — a vampire's charmed intactness —
bound in red leatherette with a gilt border,
snugged shut by a strap that snapped into
a tiny lock whose even tinier keyhole
pursed its faux-brass lips to whisper, "Pssst!
I've got a secret!" It was unignorable.

The key was lost. She snipped the strap neatly
with scissors she'd been using to cut twine,
and slid herself down grimly to the floor,
her back against a blanket chest, to survey
this relic of herself at seventeen.
But there was little here, she soon found out,
about herself in isolation: Mother
vied with her for the spotlight in most scenes
and almost always took the villain's part.
The fumes of acrimony almost choked her.
To read this, you'd have thought that adolescence
was a seven years' war. And wasn't it?
She could remember, as she hadn't wished to,
how often doors were slammed and voices raised,
or meals sat through in disapproving silence
as glacial as the silence now established
in rooms with sheet-draped furniture downstairs.
What had they fought about? What hadn't they?
Clothes, curfews, company, career,
all boiled down to combat. Would it have been
better or worse if Father hadn't died
just before these hostilities ensued?
Above the fray, he never had to take sides.
There was nothing about *him* written down
since — obviously — he couldn't be complained of,
or complained to. This was a grievance book,
pure and simple. Happy times (there were some)
had slipped by unrecorded. And it ended

in anger, as it hadn't done in life.
In recent years they'd got along beautifully
by phone, by mail, by semi-annual visits
both of them valued. Distance was the key.
You'd never guess how well we made it up,
she thought, plodding through to the last page
where a last sentence stammered still with rage:
"Why can't she ever let me lead my own life?"

The wish was granted. Doubly granted now.
Her foot had gone to sleep. She stood and felt
its numbness augered through with pins and needles
like a sewn gash split open. All she needed
now to do was lug these boxes down
to swell the discard pile (praise the Lord,
trash pickup was tomorrow). On the landing
she glanced out at a barren autumn sky
an hour before sunset. In her own house
a time zone away, less empty, equally silent,
goldfish swivelled and lunged and nipped at sprinkled
tidbits (lucky to have obliging neighbors),
casting a flash as lights turned themselves on.

NIGHTFALL, JULY 4

We have to wait until it's dark enough.
And so we settle down, spreading our blanket
on the broad slope behind the softball diamond,
looking down at the school closed for summer,
in front of which a little band sits huffing
Sousa marches through its crackling amps.
A vendor in a red, white, and blue shirt
wanders between blankets selling Sno-cones
and plastic tubes that glow a bright chartreuse
when something chemical goes on inside them.
They must have a trade name: we call them "light sticks."
Only now I heard the subliminal pun:
the things are just about the length of what
the cops, when we were children, called their night sticks —
neat little clubs they twirled walking the beat.
They whistled, too, if they were in the comics,
and sometimes maybe even in real life.
This is a safe crowd. The one noticeable
policeman's down the street directing traffic.
Antsy children jouncing these poison green
devices aren't getting much of a charge
out of their cold, pent-up fluorescence yet:
they have to wait until it's dark enough.

It's a small town, we see people we know
on all sides: next to us sits the man
who reads our gas meter, who is now
discouraging his sons from truncheoning
each other with their light sticks. It's a long
exercise of patience while the band
tootles away, halfhearted, in the finally
cooling air. We catch the merging scents
of cut grass, bug repellent, barbecues.
My children haven't grown into this school.
I come here once a year on a colder day
to vote, and once a year, as now, to see this
spectacle for which it isn't yet
dark enough — or is it? The enigmatic
firemen, their truck parked near the backstand,
are in what looks like a decisive huddle.

Disbanding, they fall back to watch the chief
ignite the first long fuse. It's dark enough.

These are New England fireworks, not lavish,
shot off singly, meant to be savored singly.
All eyes track the barely visible
ascending streak, then shimmer with reflected
spangles of explosion while a dutiful
chorus of sighs goes up: "Oooh." "Aaah."
A few babies let out first-time wails.
Looking over the captured, carnival-lit
faces of these several hundred townsfolk
I wonder just how many of them bothered
to come down here last fall and vote. The gaudy,
sulfurous, disintegrating blooms
seem every year to spring from shallower roots,
rioting over fast-eroding soil. . . .

Rioting rather tamely, one should say,
the one-by-one parade of pretty bursts
ticking off twenty minutes. But at last
they send up a whole batch together, packing
sky with blustering dazzle and reports
like a two-minute artillery barrage.
Then it is all over, sharp fumes drifting
off to disperse as finally as the flares did.
Even the green light from the children's toys
has faded — though a few, discarded, wink
up from the grass like feeble giant glowworms.
We have waited these two hundred years and more
for it to get dark enough to witness
this epilogue — a thousand points of light
fizzling over a trampled field where every
citizen winces on his own patch of blanket,
clutching his children, hoping the firemen have
a good fix on which way the wind is blowing,
until the last sparks die over the heads
of the enfranchised. Now, left in the dark,
we fill it up as best we can with a cheer.

WIND AT NIGHT

A frigid midnight. For a few
slow moments, sleep eluding us,
we lie belabored by the sad,
decamping, down-and-out nomad
who makes the dark vociferous
with notice of his passing through.

As though to pangs of flesh and bone
attuned, and aching to appal,
that hapless voice so mortifies
the wincing shingles with its cries
it could well be the voice of all
the worst bereft our time has known.

Could we have thought, at this late date,
that turning pages quickly past
the planet's rash of little wars
would leave us undistrubed indoors?
When news is bad it travels fast.
Listen, it rattles at the gate,

a century's toll of traded woe.
When will it stop? We never hear,
but drift disheartened into sleep
with one storm-wearied house to keep
or to be kept by, out of fear.
Exempt, it seems, from this one blow.

STILL LIFES

I. BELT ON BUREAU

Surely it must be asleep. And camouflaged,
brown against brown, although its grain,
more delicate, can't match the wood's precisely.

It lies in a loose coil, relaxed, but self-protective.
The immemorial shape of menace and potential.
There, at the center of its limp constriction,

you can make out most of its brazen head,
the stiff prong of a tongue now tasting nothing.
Every morning it waits to be tamed anew,

and you have long since learned its proper handling:
threading it backwards through the accustomed bands,
tricking it yet once more into biting its own tail.

II. EYEGLASSES ON NIGHT TABLE

From where you are in bed,
these are a little difficult to see.
Two ponds, it seems, adjacent; and because
their ovals are identically irregular, they must
be artificial. They are also
eerily still, quiet as earliest morning
now surrounding them. Could they be frozen?
If so, it's with the thinnest skin of ice.
If you move closer,
you can see better the ersatz-Oriental
bridge, a little arc of bronze, that joins them.
(And that is truly strange: a bridge between
a pair of ponds, not over either of them.)
You can see too some slender metal shafts
lying calm at the bottom (at each bottom),
resting at angles so naively
mirroring each other that you yearn
for something, anything, to violate
the manic symmetry of the design.
At last you see: the lefthand pond is deeper.
(Or could it be the ice is faintly thicker?)
Light bounces off it with a different,
denser glare. You blink; you realize
all these shifts of focus can be murder on the eyes.

THE POST OFFICE MURALS RESTORED

I'm tempted to want company to work with,
the emptiness becomes so eerie sometimes.
Locked in here after hours, clattering up
my ladder to refurbish this long, dim,
lofty room I feel like the one soul
in church on a weekday (truly!) with the grilled
stamp counters filling one longer wall
like a row of unemployed confessionals,
and in place of icons, posters aimed
at stamp collectors, plus the steelier ones
reminding boys to register for the just-now-
non-existent draft, or publicizing
mug shots and fingerprints of racketeers
wanted in half-a-dozen states for mail fraud.

Mail is the point. This is a post office lobby,
I tell myself. This painted wall I'm dabbing
a mild solution of detergent on
isn't *The Last Supper*. It isn't even
anything I'd choose to paint myself —
earnest, public-minded Thirties stuff —
but the artist knew what he was after
and, within limits (time and space, the ones
we all butt heads against), I'd say he got it.
In the few places where it's flaked away
to plaster my best guesses match his palette;
but for the most part it's a task of sponging,
praying the paint won't be perverse enough
to come off with the dull gray surface film.
His paint hangs firm; it rarely needs retouching.
Local color's alive under this local
dirt deposited by half-a-century's
cycles of winter soot and summer dust
heaved out in sighs by all who stood in line,
often wishing they could mail themselves
to where their packages would soon be going.
Jingling change in pockets, shifting weight
from one to another foot, how often did they
notice the frieze of vistas on three sides
of the room, filling space between the stone
dado and the ceiling, most of it

above eye level? Undoubtedly they saw it,
once or twice. And then, year after year,
they didn't see it. That's the way it is
with mural: make it fill the wall, it might
just as well be wallpaper. Better shrink it
and put a gilded frame around it if
you're reaching for that partly baffled hush
people assume at times in front of pictures.

What we have here is, in all, five pictures:
one on each of the shorter two side walls,
and three on the front wall broken by two windows
and the door in between that you come in by.
Coming in, of course, you don't see art
but those almighty counters that I mentioned
and, when the place is open, listless clerks,
happy only that they aren't the ones
carrying all that mail they weigh and cancel.
But if you look from side to side you'll see
a pair of facing scenes, a fated couple:
on the right, Agriculture (the real name
of this one, I'm afraid, is *Fruits of the Earth*)
and, on the left, Industry, more dryly titled
The Old Sawmill. I took these two on first,
leaving the long wall with the door and windows
to fuss with later. Once I got to know them
I gave them nicknames — Ag and Ind — and found
Ind the more interesting to look at, Ag
a subtler thing to clean.

                    Ag shows a hill farm
in, I suppose, late summer, early autumn —
men are making hay in the lower right-
hand corner while the balance of the scene
is apple orchard. Big children climb ladders
while younger ones fill baskets with the windfalls.
We must be watching from a higher hill
or, like the apple-pickers, from a tree,
because the land falls back before us sloping
down even as our eyes climb higher till
the top right corner's brought us to the river

curled in like a finger crooked to beckon
the children from the trees, men from the fields.
That message hasn't gotten to them yet.
A woman in a white apron carries lunch
in a cloth-covered bucket to the hayers.
(The children no doubt sample enough apples
as not to need a meal.) It reddens me
to say it, but my delicatest care
couldn't prevent this woman's apronstrings'
dissolving at my cotton wad's fine touch.
My thinnest brush tied on the bow again,
and only I can tell. Of all the scenes
this is the simplest, but it became
absorbing once I found how many different
tints of green were underneath the grime,
from olive drab to lemon-lime chartreuse,
shadowing or highlighting a dominant
shade like the back sides of dollar bills.
(Sad, when you think how little money ever
came out of all this varied verdancy.)
The range of shading makes it less a bed quilt,
although the apples all are one unnuanced
fire engine red, and the people look
stitched in place, too static even to plod.
I think the lack of animation may
have been a planned effect, a way to hint
that here is life outside of history,
even outside of time, except for that
allotted by the seasons in their round.
You can't quite tell when any of this takes place:
the clothes are nondescript, no cars or wagons
crowd the river road. We can say only
farms like this one aren't to be found these days.

Nor is the old sawmill. This, by contrast,
offers some movement: the men working bend
with the weight of logs they shoulder, tote, and shove
into the steam-driven frenzy of the saw.
It is a great, airy, barnlike place,
with a wide-open door, through which we see
the timber wagon only half unloaded,

and an enormous, pallid heap of sawdust
kept dry under a rickety canopy. (It must
have been a product somebody would buy.)
The wagon road winds down to the same river
we saw in the farm scene, but notice, here
we're on the river's other bank, its bend
swerves outward now, more like a question mark.
Beyond, among the hills, are huddled farms
like the one we've just seen, and see no more,
that as they failed sent men down here to work.

Although in real life they'd be bored to death,
these wage-slaves are more interesting to look at
than the agrarian icons: there's the boy
of junior high school age sweeping up sawdust,
whose face needed some washing, as you'd well
expect it might on such a job as that.
Since I've gone at it (tensely, with a Q-tip)
his cheek beams forth with such a healthy tint
it would be hard to label him exploited.
Better sawdust than chalk dust, he might say.
And there's the man on a break whittling a scrap
of wood into a doll for his daughter at home.
(Imagine how she'd say, "But where's the face?"
And he, not irritated, patient, saying,
"That's the best that I could do with that
old knife of mine. You got to draw the face on.")
What makes it more dynamic, though, is not
the figures in themselves — they're pretty stiff —
but the brisk forms they gravitate around.
Bore through the human interest and you find
circles: ironbound wheels of the wagon, fanged,
flashing wheel that is the big saw's blade,
and, not least, a great log's severed end
that faces us, clean, papery, and showing
plainly immense age. You can count its rings,
wheels within wheels that sped it to a time
when wheels would spin to bring the forests down.
Once this amount of motion is brought into it,
it's only a short step on to history.
Here, it's literally a quarter-turn,

which brings you face to face with the long wall,
full of lore to ponder on your way out.

There, as I've said, you're favored with a triptych:
a painting framing each of the two windows,
and one that flanks and crowns the heavy glass
door at the center. Would-be classical
pilasters section off these three vignettes —
it's a bit busy. Where to begin? The left,
I guess, which goes back even to pre-history,
that is, before the founding of the town.
It's of a forest clearing where a pair
of fur traders socialize with Indians.
Some small thing (a rabbit?) roasts on a spit,
and the men share a pipe beside the fire,
all wearing deerskin, though the Indians
wear less of it. It's what we'd call nowadays
a working lunch, because the trading items
are spread out waiting to be haggled over:
bearskins and beaver pelts one red man points
a finger at, while studying the beads
one of the traders holds up for inspection.
Strand on strand of colored glass; and more
spills from the open flap of the leather bag.
That isn't all: there are some useful tools
ready for swapping — needles and small knives.
No rum or guns, at least. It's fairly wholesome.
And yet . . . was there a moment by the fire
when both sides could have made a better deal?
Dabbing it clean by inches I was bothered
by weird sensations, as if I could feel
the textures changing hands in these transactions.
The red men handed over something warm
and soft, and got in payment something cold
and hard. They couldn't possibly have known
what they were buying into, any more
than they or their pale guests could have divined
that this unbroken wilderness they sat in
would in a century and a bit be axed.
The trees were fair game once the game was gone.

It could be I impose the ominous tone.
Look without thinking too much and you see
something innocuous as boy scout camp.
At the far right, though, is a view that doesn't
force you to work at reading danger into it.
This is a night arrival at a station
of the Underground Railroad. Runaway slaves
bend double, scuffling down the cellar steps
of the red-bearded parson who became
a local legend: here he is, presiding,
grim in his clericals with a covered lantern,
holding his cellar hatch up for the last
passengers that hustle through his barnyard,
trying to beat the moon before it rises
over the cloud it just peeps out from now.
The scant, worrying light it sends down hits
the parson's face, set in an anxious scowl,
showing more plainly than the faces of
his no doubt equally anxious overnight guests.
If not their features, plenty of their fear
comes through in the forward lunge of bodies
into the battened safety of that hole.
This Henry Ward Beecher of the provinces
stuck by his own moonlighting, shunting hundreds
in here and out, and off to Canada.
These blacks are in every sense just passing through.
There are no blacks in town now that I know of.
(Nor, you'll be thinking, any Indians. Right.)

Finally I'm at the final scene, the aegis
under which all must come in and go out.
I've set my ladder up astride the door;
if we were open and you wanted stamps
you'd have to risk bad luck and weasel under it.
(Another reason to do this job at night.)
Of all the paintings this is the most crowded,
and yet it seems of all of them the most quiet.
Memorial Day is what it's called. It gives
a view of the town green, a small triangle
of grass and a few trees and a generic
Union Soldier's statue at the center.

It's a mass gathering, a chance to wear
a uniform if you have one, or just dress up,
parading to and from the cemetery,
ending up here, after the wreaths are laid,
for the Mayor's speech, more drumrolls, more salutes.
See how they stand in neat rows round the statue
like the redeemed that throng a reredos
before the Throne of Grace: the Volunteer
Fire Department, all six of them, and one
policeman standing close behind the Mayor;
schoolchildren holding tiny flags and staring
at all the former doughboys who've been home
now for more than a decade from the War
to End All Wars. One's missing an arm. Many
show a middle-aged spread. They all stand tall
in khaki for a day. This is how things were
when it was painted, fifty years or so
ago, and it is here that history
comes to an end in this small town P.O.
Silence and night press in against me now.
Try as I will, I can't dream up the sound
of the small band, of the determined voices
singing "There's a long, long trail a-winding,"
nor of the huffed, triumphal rhetoric
disgorged beneath the statue's stony trance.
This one-armed man I'm sponging off looks happy,
as they all do — just happy to be home.
When I go home myself, fold up my ladder,
and leave by this glass door for the last time,
I'll notice as I always do the neat stroke
of wit the artist realized in his placing
a view of the town center *at* the center:
for, whenever I step outside, I see
in front of me the place itself: the grass
triangle with its statue just the same,
most of the same trees (though some elms are gone)
and the same modest downtown row of stores,
shabbier now, some seven recessions later.

To go out from his painting, then, should be
to step inside it, to become a part

of what you've just been looking at. It must
have made the townsfolk back then smile and think,
"This place is ours, inside and out," and think
that even the worst troubles might be managed.
I wish it were that easy, every night
when I lock up and walk across the green
to midpoint where, feeling myself inspected,
I slow my pace under the sentry's granite
stare from his high pedestal — too high
for me to look him staightly in the eye,
as I have done so often with his twin
inside, up on my ladder. College boys
who, when they're home for Christmas every year,
sneak out at night to crown him with a ski cap
have met his level gaze on his own level.
I can no more make out his hard young face
than I can see that of the figure slumped
across the street in the bus shelter, where
he's found himself a home to last the night.
What made our muralist omit that sight
and others like it which his Great Depression
furnished in plenty was, I'm now persuaded,
not a genteel aversion to the worst
sores and unrest a nation had to show
but a belief that they would not be lasting,
a flash of confidence. Why can't we share it?
Too much has happened since those old hard times.
Three wars and fifty-odd Memorial Days
after the painter laid his brush down, I
take pains to cleanse and blot his bristling strokes
that aimed to smooth the wrinkles of the world,
and inch by inch unveil their earliest gleam.
But walking home through streets that night has emptied
in this small town that's never come to much,
those heartening hues are hard to bear in mind.
I see cast over all what I would paint
if I were ever given the commission:
that dinginess hope leaves when it deserts us,
that smudge of squandered opportunity.